SCAMS & HYPOCRISY

The Cancer of Our Age

Scams

&

Hypocrisy

THE CANCER OF OUR AGE

D. P. MARCHESSINI

ASKELON PUBLISHING

Askelon Publishing
PO Box 29153 London SW1X 8WD

Published by Askelon Publishing 2010

2 4 6 8 10 9 7 5 3 1

ISBN 978-0-9564622-0-6

Copyright © 2010 D. P. Marchessini

Printed in the United Kingdom

Preface

We are living in a unique era of history, when the level of hypocrisy throughout the world is unprecedented. Of course, there has been hypocrisy since the beginning of time, but there has also been mockery and shafts of truth which have punctured the hypocrisy. Today, there is no mockery or truth. Everyone believes whatever the government tells them and, indeed, anyone who contradicts the government is attacked and persecuted. This is especially true in the Anglo-Saxon world of the United States and England. No doubt, one of the factors is political correctness, which does not allow either contradiction or mockery. And there is also the proliferation of the media, so that people are bombarded from all sides by lies.

The intention of this book is to prick some of the more outrageous hypocrisies.

Contents

Arkansas truth

At a certain time, while Bill Clinton was Governor of Arkansas, drugs began to be smuggled into western Arkansas, the most remote part of the State. This smuggling was done by plane. Planes are rather difficult to conceal, so all the State Troopers were well aware of what was going on. Nevertheless, no attempt was made to stop the smuggling. Some years later, it was finally ascertained that the man who was in charge of this drug smuggling was a Mr Dan Lasater. And who was Mr Lasater? Mr Lasater was Mr Clinton's business partner in Little Rock. He later made himself famous when he said before a Congressional Committee, "What is wrong with bringing in drugs if you don't charge for them?". Yet Clinton did not come in for any criticism for this matter. He was not even mentioned.

In the Arkansas of the Clintons, there were a lot of bribes floating around. The Clintons accepted bribes, but they also gave bribes. There was a two-way traffic. Clinton had a bodyguard and chauffeur called L.D.

Brown, who was treated as one of the family, and who was frequently consulted for advice by both Clintons. After leaving the Clintons, L.D. Brown wrote a book called "Crossfire", which was non-political, and simply detailed his life with the Clintons. Among other things, Brown revealed that he had been Clinton's "bag man". One of Clinton's methods was to give money to black ministers, who then made sure that all their black parishioners voted for Clinton. The Whitewater investigation was informed that L.D. Brown was Clinton's "bag man", and he was interrogated. But, of course, nothing came of it. The Clintons also accepted bribes. Brown also revealed that one money spinner was "Fund Raisers". Under Federal laws, no one was allowed to give more than $1,000 to any political party or candidate. It was, therefore, necessary to assemble a large group of people in order to get a sizeable amount of money. Clinton found it easy to obtain a large number of donors to contribute, because they were assured that they would get their money back. One very rich backer would then give Clinton the total amount "raised", and all the official donors would be reimbursed. Perhaps the most famous bribe was the $100,000 that Mrs Clinton received through a "Commodity Account". It is public knowledge that Mrs Clinton put $1,000 in the Account and, in six weeks, received $100,000 back from her broker. Now, no one in the world is clever enough to be able to do that, but if there were somebody who could do that, he would be sitting on his yacht in the Mediterranean, not sitting in a small brokerage office in Little Rock, Arkansas. But the story was even worse. The records of all Hillary's trades show that they were all in Cattle Futures. At the time, the cattle market was in the biggest bull market it had ever had. One might therefore be excused for thinking that Hillary just got lucky and rode the coat-tails of the bull market. But, in fact, all of Mrs Clinton's trades were SHORT. In other words, she made one hundred times her money, going short in an enormous bull market. Even a small child would not believe that.

Hillary had a big love affair with Vince Foster, who was one of her law partners, and also the Clintons' lawyer. Wild Bill also had a mistress in Little Rock, a lady called Beth Coulson, who was the only high-class woman in his life. The Clintons accepted each other's lovers, and would often dine together. Little Rock is a small town and these things were well-known. Mrs Clinton and Vince Foster bought a cabin together in the woods near Little Rock, and would often go and spend the night there. They would also travel together, and once even went to London together. What Mrs Clinton did object to was what she called "extra-marital sex". In particular, Wild Bill often would go cruising at night, with L.D. driving him. They would go to a bar or disco, where Bill would point out a girl that he fancied. L.D. would then go up to her and say "How would you like to dance with the Governor of Arkansas?". Most of the time the girls did want to, with L.D. watching. After some preparatory dancing, Wild Bill would take the wretched girl out to the back and have her suck his cock. Very elegant and refined behaviour. This was often discussed with L.D.

After Clinton got to Washington, things became much worse. Thirty-five of his business associates and/or political allies were indicted for fraud, and three were murdered. This was unprecedented in the Presidential history of the United States. Another crime that Clinton committed was to cover up the murder of Vince Foster, who was his lawyer and only friend. Foster's body was found in a Washington park, lying flat, in an unnatural stiff position. He was lying on the grass several hundred yards from any pavement, yet his shoes did not have any grass or mud on them. He owned a gun, but the gun in his hand was not his own gun. Where was his own gun? His hand was around the trigger in such a contorted way that it would have been impossible to fire the gun. The bullet hole in his throat did not coincide with the gun in his hand. There were many more details, making it clear that his death could not be suicide. Did Clinton appoint the FBI to investigate the matter? No he did not. Well, did he appoint the Washington D.C. Police to investigate the matter? No, he did not. He appointed the Washington Park Police, whose only previous experience was breaking up canoodling couples, and who had never investigated a murder before. The poor Park Police even forgot to look for the bullet. When they went back, three weeks later, it was gone. When they went to the White House to search Foster's office, they were not allowed in by the White House Counsel, Bernie Nussbaun, until his own minions had hoovered the office and made sure there was nothing in it derogatory to the Clintons. This became well-known. The amazing thing was that the Republicans, who had a majority in Congress, did not do anything about this. They just sat on their hands and let him get away with it. There was an uproar later, but it was too late. The committee that was formed to investigate was too futile, and the White House staff stone-walled behind Clinton. One White House secretary, who was questioned, used the phrase "I don't remember" 178 times during her testimony.

But Clinton was not finished yet. He still had the Lewinsky scandal to come, when he was caught committing perjury. Of course, only a child would believe that Lewinsky was the only White House intern that Clinton had his hands on. She was the ugliest of the lot, and it would be impossible for Clinton not to have had contact with the more attractive ones as well.

Indeed, one of them was seen buttoning her blouse as she came out of his office. Perjury is a Federal crime for which one goes to jail. A lady in Texas, who was tried about the same time as Clinton, had to go to jail for doing exactly the same thing. Clinton not only did not go to jail, but he remained President, and although he was impeached by the House of Representatives, the Senate did not ratify the impeachment. This was shocking to Europeans. It was Third World behaviour.

But the most shocking action that Clinton committed took place on his very last day in office, when he pardoned Marc Rich, the well-known fugitive. Now, Clinton was not related to Marc Rich — he was not his brother, nor his cousin. Indeed, he had never even met him. Why, therefore, would he pardon a well-known fugitive? It is perfectly obvious that Rich must have given him an enormous bribe. And yet this possibility has never been raised in America. American naïvety is amazing, and Clinton relied on it. He knew that he would get away with it.

The truth is never racist

At the 1988 Olympics in Korea, there was a spectacular photograph of the finish of the 100 metre dash. It was taken from behind the finish line, so that the eight finalists were running towards the camera. All eight finalists were black. The odds of this being a coincidence would be in the trillions, but we all already knew that blacks run faster than whites. They have been dominating athletics events for many years.

Apart from athletics, they also dominate many other sports. In the National Basketball Association, in America, 86% of the players are black, although only 13% of Americans are black. In football, the story is similar. In the National Football League the vast majority of players are also black. In other words, blacks are simply better athletes - they can run faster; they can jump higher; they are bigger and stronger. Although this is perfectly obvious, very few people mention it, because it is not "Politically Correct". What the Politically Correct people are afraid of admitting is that, if the blacks are different to whites physically, then they may be different mentally. This question of comparative IQs is always discussed on the basis of white versus black. That is not at all the point.

The fact is that not only does every race has a different IQ, but even every country has a different IQ. IQ tests have shown that the Orientals in general, and the Chinese in particular, are the most intelligent race. The reason they are the most intelligent race is because they have the longest civilisation behind them — 5,000 years. After them, come the Indians and Pakistanis. Then come the whites. The difference between the Chinese and the whites is approximately ten percent, which is enormous. Among the whites, the cleverest are the Jews - they have had a long civilisation behind them. Among Europeans, the cleverest are the Greeks, because they have had the longest civilisation in Europe. The least intelligent are the Portuguese, who have had a very short civilisation. The blacks, according to many IQ tests, have IQ ten percent below the whites. They have had very little civilisation. If the blacks had had 5,000 years of civilisation, like the Chinese, no doubt they would be as intelligent as the Chinese. Below the blacks, at the bottom of the ladder, are Red Indians.

But just as there are differences between races,

there are many differences between countries. Why are the most beautiful love songs Spanish? — have you ever heard of a Swedish love song? Why are the greatest operas Italian? Why are most great composers German, and most great chess players Slav? Why are most great novels English, or French. Bulgaria is a small country, but, at every Olympics, it wins gold medals in weight-lifting. In the grand hotels in Europe before the War, the waiters in the dining room were always Italian, because they were the most charming. But the waiters in Room Service were all German — because they never forgot anything. There was a recent survey about the incidence of anger among European countries. The Italians got angry an average 3½–5 times a day. The Danes got angry once every 10 days. Are they the same?

To pretend that there is no difference between races and countries is simply hypocrisy. It is only by recognising the differences, and working on the lower categories, that the human race can be improved.

PLO or KGB?

Of all the political subjects that come up regularly in the newspapers, the one that appears most often is the continuous fighting between Israel and the PLO. Instead of putting forward arguments on this subject, I would like to bring to your attention only some facts — and leave you to come to your own conclusions.

In 1947, the United Nations produced a Partition Plan which would have created two viable States — one Jewish and one Arab — in Palestine. The Jews accepted the United Nations Plan, but the Arabs did not. As a result, Israel declared its independence in 1948.

Immediately after Israel had declared independence, all the Arab States declared war on Israel. The Arab States then advised all Palestinian Arabs to leave Israel, in order that they would not be in the way when the fighting took place. No Arabs, however, were asked to leave by the Jews, and there are still many Arabs living in Israel. Since then, the Arab states have declared four wars on Israel altogether, all of which they have lost. All of the wars were financed by Saudi Arabia, who claims to be neutral. The Arab States forcibly ejected all Jews from Arab countries, a total of almost a million people.

When the PLO was established, one of the clauses in its Charter called for the expulsion of all Jews from Israel. Although the PLO have verbally agreed to delete this clause from their Charter, they have never done so. The term "Palestinians" is disingenuous. It suggests that the Arabs are Palestinians and the Jews are not. But if Palestinian means a native of Palestine, there are many Jews who have been natives of Palestine for centuries. In short, there are Jewish Palestinians as well as Arab Palestinians.

There have been several attempts made to move the Palestinians out of the camps. On each occasion, the Arab leaders refused to allow the Palestinian Arabs to be moved, despite the poverty and discomfort in which they lived, in order to keep political pressure on Israel and the United States. Nor do the Arabs allow the Palestinians to become citizens of any of their countries.

In a recent poll taken of Palestinian Arabs, over 70% said they had no desire to return to Israel. The results of this poll so infuriated Arab terrorists that they destroyed the offices of the company who had done the survey, and beat up its employees.

General Pacepa of Rumania was the highest ranking intelligence officer ever to have defected from the Soviet Block. He has written in the Wall Street Journal that Arafat was a KGB agent who worked under him and was also an active terrorist. It was the KGB who made Arafat Chairman of the PLO. Indeed, Arafat was not even a Palestinian, but an Egyptian. Apart from heading the PLO, Arafat was also head, since 1957, of al-Fatah, the Palestinian terror organisation.

There are no Israeli suicide bombers, but there are plenty of Arab bombers.

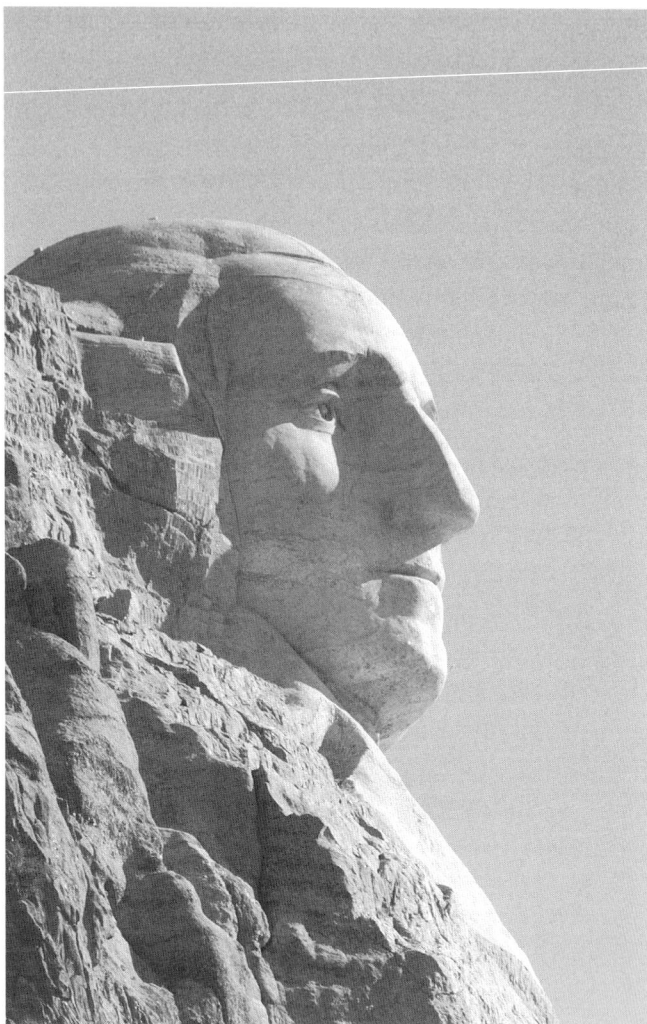

What price democracy?

Although everyone continues to use the phrase "democracy", and it is considered by many people to be the best form of government, it is interesting to consider how many genuine democracies there are in the world today. To begin with, history has shown that a republic is usually a much more successful form of government than a democracy. Rome and Venice are good examples of successful republics. The difference is that, in a republic, people do not vote directly for candidates — they vote for electors who then choose the candidates. Switzerland is a Republic today and, compared to the countries of the West, it is much better run. The United States is also officially a Republic, because the Founding Fathers did not think the average man would be able to choose between presidential candidates. They therefore wrote the Constitution, so that the voting would be for Electors, (distinguished people from each State), who would then choose the President. This sounds rather sensible, but it was negated by the political parties, who put up slates of Electors already committed to a party in advance. In effect, this turned the United States into a democracy. However, the Electors still have the legal right to vote for anyone they wish to. Some years ago, some of the Southern Electors voted for Senator Strom Thurmond as President, even though he was not running. England is also not, strictly speaking, a democracy, because of the House of Lords. Even after Asquith took much of the power away from the Lords in 1911, the House of Lords continues to have both prestige and influence.

As regards the rest of Europe, the picture is not encouraging. After 14 years of democracy, the Germans produced Hitler. In 1958, the French politicians were unable to govern France any longer. They threw up their hands and called for De Gaulle. Spain has had a chequered career of democracies, monarchies and Civil Wars, as has Greece. Italy has, theoretically, been a democracy since the War, but it has proportional representation, making it hard to govern. That is probably why they have done so well. Eastern Europe has been either under the Nazis or under the Communists, until recently. In the Middle East, there are no democracies. There are Socialist dictatorships of various kinds. And that is also the case in Egypt. In the Black African countries, democracy is a joke. They are either dictatorships or one-party states. When someone once mentioned the slogan "One Man, One Vote" to Ian Smith, the Rhodesian Prime Minster, he replied "Yes, but in Africa, it is: One Man, One Vote, One Time".

One country where democracy seems to have worked since the War is Japan, perhaps because the Japanese are more disciplined. In the South American countries, dictatorships alternate with Communist governments. Brazil makes an effort to be a democracy, but corruption is rampant. Some years ago, a well-known Brazilian politician was caught stealing, and had to leave the country. Surprisingly, he not only came back some years later, but ran for political office again. His election slogan was: "He steals, but he is efficient" — he was elected. In Mexico, it is even worse. Many years ago, a friend of mine had a romance with a Mexican girl, whose father was a Minister in the government. After six months in office, he resigned. My friend asked the girl why her father had resigned after such a short time. She said "In Mexico, in six months, one can steal as much as one needs. There is no point to stay on.".

And yet the Americans think that democracy can be established in any country in ten minutes. They do not grasp that, for a democracy, you need not only an educated population, but political traditions and principles that have existed for many years. The idea of establishing a democracy in Iraq, where there were three separate groups of people - all of them hostile to each other — was particularly insane.

But is it tennis?

One often sees articles in the sports pages complaining that tennis nowadays has become dull and stereotyped, and lamenting the absence of "colourful" characters like McEnroe and Connors. The truth is that McEnroe and Connors did not make tennis exciting — in the '50s and '60s when tennis really was exciting, there were no McEnroes or Connors. The reason that tennis today has become dull is that the game that the top players' play is not really tennis — it is a perfectly good game, but it is not tennis.

The word "tennis" is, of course, short for Lawn Tennis. As its name implies, Lawn Tennis was invented for, and meant to be played on, grass. For the first one hundred years of its existence, all the major tournaments were on grass, except for the French Open. As a result, the best players always won. Today, it is the opposite way around: the only major grass tournament left is Wimbledon, and even that has been watered down. The courts have been made softer, and the balls have been made lighter, making the courts less like traditional grass, and more like slow courts. Why is tennis no longer played on grass? For the usual reason — money. Grass courts are more difficult to build, more expensive to maintain, and can only be used in the summer. The tennis season, which used to extend only from April to September (apart from Australia), now has big money tournaments twelve months a year, almost all of which are televised. It is, therefore, necessary to have hard courts and artificial indoor courts. (It is difficult to exaggerate the importance of television — it provides most of the money with which the players are paid, and gives the exposure that the advertisers want. As a result, everything is arranged to suit television's convenience.)

What is not widely appreciated, however, is to what extent the change in surfaces has altered the game. Apart from the tradition of grass, the beauty of grass, and the fact that grass is much easier on the players' feet, the grass surface is also vital to the quality of the strokes. As long ago as the 1920s, Bill Tilden, perhaps the greatest and certainly the most intelligent tennis player of all time, pointed out that good players rarely hit flat shots, because they are unreliable; they hit almost every shot with spin — either topspin or underspin. Grass is the only surface on which these two spins are equally effective. The game is thus evenly balanced .

On clay and other slow surfaces, underspin is useless because the ball sits up; on very fast surfaces, there is not enough time to put topspin on the ball. It is only on grass that both spins can be used effectively, and thereby create the variety of stroke play which makes the game vastly richer and more interesting.

Today, even at Wimbledon, because the grass has been made softer and the balls lighter, players rarely rush the net. This is despite the fact that, some years ago, the service rule was altered, so that the server is allowed to have one leg over the service line before he hits the ball, which, in effect, gains him one step in getting to the net. What kind of grass court tennis is that — without net rushing? A result of the new equipment is that it enables the players to hit the ball much faster on any surface, and has consequently caused the margin between the top players and the others to narrow. (As Rod Laver once said, "In the days of the wooden racquet, one had to be quite talented to play well.") The result has been more speed, less skill. When combined with the continuous changes in tournament surfaces, it has caused tournament results to become haphazard and inconsistent, with the top players frequently losing to unknowns.

One is often told how much better the players of today are than those of two generations ago. What people mean, of course, is that, because of the money and the equipment, there are many more good players playing on the circuit today than there were forty years ago. There were then many fewer tournaments and less than twenty strong players. The player who is 200th in the computer rankings today would easily beat all but the top 20 players of forty years ago. But if Federer or Nadal were to play against Laver at his peak with wooden racquets, who would win? Would the best players of today have beaten Tilden, Budge, Kramer or Sedgman at their peak with the same equipment?

There is also the distasteful phenomenon that players today are allowed to cheat. The Rules of Tennis clearly state that "play shall be continuous". Each time that a player stops play to contest a ruling, therefore, he is not only being discourteous and unsportsmanlike, but he is also breaking the rules of Tennis. The leading culprit was McEnroe. Not surprisingly, players very rarely stop to argue about a line call when they are winning — it seems to happen only when they are losing, and when their opponent is going well. Inevitably, the interruption disrupts their opponent's rhythm and concentration, while giving themselves a chance to re-group. That is quite clearly cheating, and yet it is allowed to continue. Is that "tennis" ?

At Wimbledon in 1949, one of the finest matches

in Wimbledon history was contested between Ted Schroeder, the pre-tournament favourite, and Frank Sedgman, who was the best player in the tournament apart from Schroeder, and who was to win the next two Wimbledons. Although it was only the Quarter-Final, it was widely considered that this match would probably decide the winner of the tournament, and so it proved. The match did not disappoint. Sedgman quickly won the first two sets, but Schroeder struck back to win the next two. In the fifth set, games followed service, and with the game score 4-5, Schroeder was serving to save the match. The score reached 30-40, which was match point to Sedgman. Schroeder then hit a tremendous service which Sedgman was unable to return, and which appeared to make the score deuce, when suddenly the baseline judge on Schroeder's side raised his hand to call a foot-fault. Schroeder had been foot-faulted on match point! It is interesting to compare his reaction with what goes on in tennis today. He did not say anything to the linesman, nor make any gesture of annoyance. He simply bounced the ball a few times, then hit a second serve, followed it to the net, and went on to win the point. He then won the game, then the match, and eventually won Wimbledon. That is what tennis is all about.

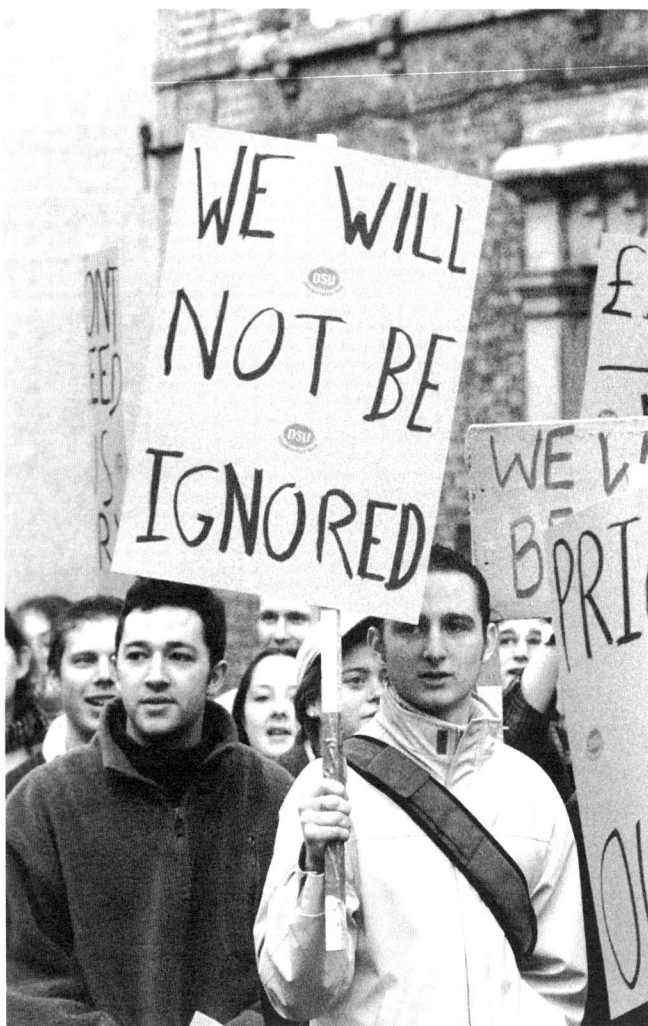

Students are dangerous

It seems that almost every time one looks in the newspapers, students are demonstrating somewhere in the world. Recently, there were many days of violent demonstrations in Greece. Now, in Greece, students are "sacred", and the Police is not even allowed to go into the universities. That means that students are priceless for those who wish to cause trouble - invariably that means the Socialists or, in Greece, the Communists. It is very easy to get young people stirred up about something, and once that is done, demonstrations can be arranged very easily. The headlines always are "Students Demonstrate", but the demonstrations are always organised and led by the Left. In Greece, there is a particularly strong Communist party. Indeed, at one time, there were three separate Communist parties. The Left use the students as a shield, because the Police are always reluctant to fire on students. At the same time, the Left obtains the credit for the students demonstrations, although the students are not necessarily demonstrating for the purposes that the Left-wing wish. One cannot have a good demonstration any more, unless one has a good quantity of students as shields.

Perhaps the most famous student demonstrations in the twentieth century were the 1968 demonstrations in Paris, which eventually toppled De Gaulle. These demonstrations are still spoken of with pride by the Left-wing, and they are sometimes referred to as "The voice of the people". France has a law like the United States whereby, after 30 years, all government documents must be opened to the public. In 1998, therefore, 30 years after the demonstrations, all the documents about them were opened. It was reported in the press that the documents had made clear that the French Security Service had been aware at the time that the demonstrations had been organised by the Cubans, and had been financed by the Russians, yet there was very little public reaction to his news. "The voice of the people" indeed.

The real McCarthy

There is a similar story in the United States. Senator McCarthy has been one of the biggest whipping boys of the Left over the last 50 years. McCarthy's great crime in the eyes of the Left was that, in the late 1940s and early 1950s, he alleged that many people working in the U.S. State Department were Soviet spies. This was considered bad behaviour, not only by the Left, but also by such people as President Harry Truman and George Marshall, the Secretary of State. McCarthy not only received no help in this matter from the U.S. Government, but he became unpopular, and was eventually hounded out of Congress.

Towards the end of the Second World War, the U.S. Secret Service (later the CIA) began a project called the Venona Project, whose purpose was to break the Russian code and eventually they succeeded in doing so. From then on, all Russian communications to the United States were read by the Secret Service. Some years later, when the programme was terminated, the documents were sent to the archives in Washington.

Now, the United States has the law that, after 30 years, all government documents must be open to the public. In 1995, therefore, Senator Daniel Moynihan, of New York, bravely insisted that the government open up the documents of the Venona Project. The results were stupefying. Every single person named by Senator McCarthy as a Soviet agent had, indeed, been a Soviet agent. But even more surprising, there had been many Soviet agents that McCarthy had not been aware of. Indeed, the State Department had been riddled with Soviet agents. Despite these facts, no one has tried to rehabilitate McCarthy's reputation. Although the Venona papers have been sporadically mentioned in the Press, even in the New York Times, no one has tried to make clear what was in them.

Hot air

One of the amazing phenomena in today's world is the belief, by a large portion of the population, that "global warming" is caused by man. There is not the slightest evidence for this belief, and yet not only do many people believe it implicitly, but they castigate and criticise as "fools" those who do not accept it. What is the evidence for this assertion?

1. At the International Scientific Conference on "Global Warming" that took place in London last year, the conference broke up with a statement that there was no scientific evidence to prove that humans can affect global warming. This result did not end the dispute about "global warming", however nor did it end the castigation of those who do not accept it.

2. Anyone who has studied the matter knows that global temperatures have been going both up and down since records have been kept. Global temperatures in the Middle Ages are known to have been higher than they are today. In the 16th and 17th centuries however

the world went through a "cold" period with much lower temperatures than normal. At the beginning of the 20th century, temperatures were warm, but between 1940 and 1970 the temperatures fell, although there was plenty of pollution. Temperatures peaked in the mid-1990s, and since the year 2000 have been falling. Is this Global Warming? Furthermore the sea, which is a very important part of "Global Warming" is NOT warming, nor has its level changed despite claims to the contrary.

Lord Monckton, who tries to show what nonsense "Global Warming" is, has challenged Mr. Al Gore to a debate on the matter. But, of course, Gore has refused, because he knows that there are many inaccuracies in the statements and videos he has made.

3. There has been a lot of publicity about how the Arctic is receding, and a lot of sympathy for the polar bears, who have to swim further to get food. What is never mentioned is that the ice mass of Antarctica has increased by eight percent in the last few years. As for the polar bears, in 1950 there were only 5,000 polar bears. Today there are 25,000. They seem to be thriving.

4. A frightening treaty called the Copenhagen Treaty has been prepared, which all the nations in the world are meant to sign in December 2009. It is very

long (perhaps deliberately to discourage people from reading it) but if one makes the effort to read it, one will find several very alarming points.

The first is that a World Government is to be established (to be controlled, of course, by the climate activists). Secondly, all the rich nations are meant to give money to all the nations who do not have favourable climates. This is almost the whole world. This will be known as "Climate Debt". Thirdly, there are measures to enforce this handover of funds.

More hot air England is ruled by a Socialist government. In Germany, the government is balanced between the Conservatives and the Socialists. In France, the Socialists ruled for a long time, and are still the largest political party in France. In Spain, the Socialists rule. There is a big Socialist Party in Italy, and Greece was ruled by the Socialists for many years. The Scandinavian countries have been Socialist for 80 years. The Middle Eastern countries are all Socialist, and India has been Socialist since its Independence. Japan has a large Socialist party, as does Australia. So do the South American countries. There is only one sizeable country in the world which does not have a Socialist Party, and that is the United States. Does that mean that there are no Socialists in the United States?

Have all Americans been inoculated with anti-Socialist serum? Of course not. America is full of Socialists.

But, because "Socialist" is still a dirty word in America, American Socialists choose to call themselves "Liberals", and they get away with this outrageous euphemism. Not only are they not Liberals, but they are opposed to the principles of the famous Liberal Party of England — the party of Gladstone and Asquith. The Liberals stood for individual rights. When the First War broke out, the Liberals were in power, and they hesitated whether or not to have conscription, because it obviously restricted individual rights. In the end, they did install mandatory conscription, but only after a lot of soul-searching. The people in the United States, who call themselves "Liberals" are, on the contrary, in favour of government intervention in daily life, and the imposition, by force, of Socialist measures. And yet they are allowed to call themselves "Liberals". What hypocrisy!

Even more hot air Another of the most hypocritical issues in today's world is the guilt about the slavery practised in the New World by the colonial powers. Americans are wringing their hands in remorse at this terrible thing. As usual, the Americans only see their own history. The fact is that slavery has existed since the beginning of time, all over the world. There was nothing new about it. The colonial powers did not invent it. More to the point, people refuse to admit that the blacks had anything to do with it. When the English and the French landed in West Africa, they did not run around with lassoes, trying to catch blacks. They bought slaves from BLACK slave dealers. Indeed, the slave trade was the mainstay of the black kingdoms of West Africa, and was what they lived on. There had always been an enormous amount of slavery throughout all of Black Africa. At one time, three-quarters of Black Africans were slaves.

Nor did slaves in Africa have a very good future. Their average life expectancy was only about six months. The voyage to America was horrible, but those who survived it had a considerably longer life expectancy. The most amusing event was that, after first England, and then France, had abolished slavery, and slave trading had fallen drastically, a delegation from West Africa came to the European capitals, to protest that their income had been cut, and to request that their abolition of slavery be reversed.

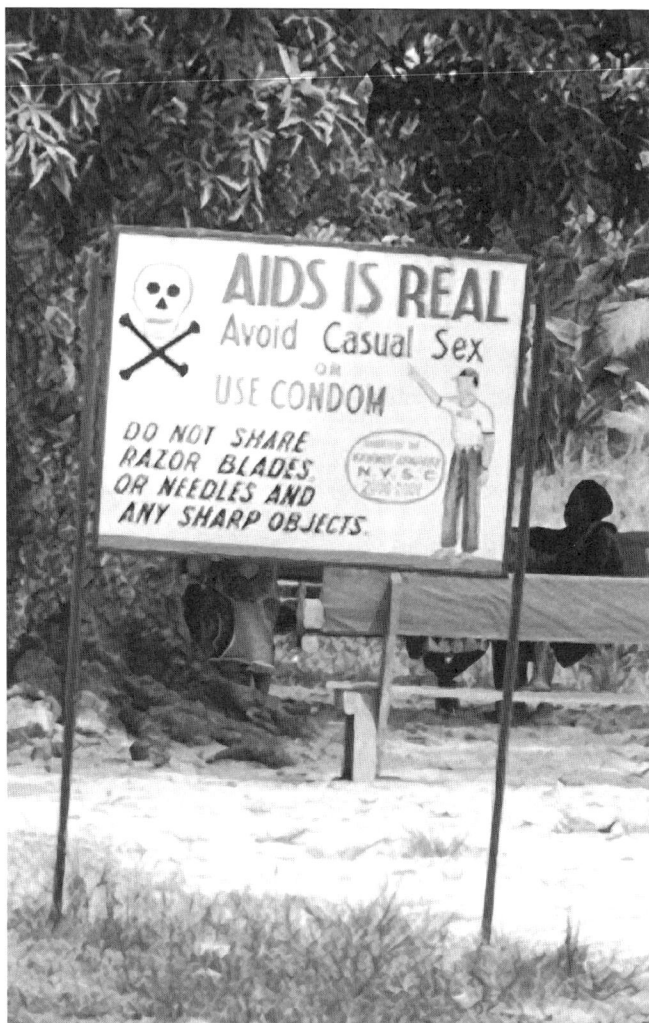

The biggest scam

Perhaps the biggest scam in the world in the last 100 years has been the myth of AIDS. AIDS is not a disease — it is a syndrome which includes about 25 diseases — the accumulation of many symptoms, resulting in the destruction of the body's resistance. This illness surfaced in the '70s, first in San Francisco, the home of the infamous homosexual "bath houses". Most of its victims, of course, were homosexuals, or drug-users. What people did not understand at that time, and most people still do not understand, is that being homosexual is the same as being a drug-user, because when homosexuals go "cruising", they pick up five, ten or 15 partners in one night. Naturally, they cannot have that many erections naturally, so they have to take drugs with names like "Thunderbolt", or "Ramrod", to get an erection. It is these drugs that destroy the body's resistance.

Although the number of people hit by AIDS was very small compared to the major diseases, the government put AIDS at the top of its list for political reasons. Finally, in 1984, the government held a press conference at which it announced that a virus called HIV "may be" the cause of AIDS. This was extraordinary. First of all, it was unheard of for a medical diagnosis to be made by the government, instead of by panels of distinguished doctors. Secondly, the HIV information was sent to the U.S. Government by the French doctor, Dr Luc Montagnier. Yet Dr Montagnier publicly admits today that HIV does not give AIDS.

Now, it was, and is, perfectly clear that HIV could not possibly be the cause of AIDS. HIV is a virus, and viruses spread like wildfire, like colds. For this reason, many people predicted, around 1980, that because of this there would be millions of AIDS deaths in the United States by the turn of the century. This prediction turned out to be ridiculous. Not only did AIDS sufferers not multiply, but their rate of increase has slowed. Furthermore, people with HIV stubbornly refused to die of AIDS. For this reason, those who believed the HIV theory assumed there must be an incubation period. At first, it was assumed to be a year. But after a year, people were still not dying of AIDS. The incubation period was then extended to five years, and later to ten years, without success. Finally, the incubation period was abandoned. Furthermore, there are many AIDS sufferers who do not have

HIV. This inconvenient fact has been abolished by the government, who now defines AIDS as "having HIV".

Needless to say, there were doctors who pointed out the above obvious facts, but they were ostracised and hounded. Most of them lost their government grants, lost their laboratory faculties, and were even banned from medical conferences. The leading opponent of the HIV theory is Peter Duesberg. Prior to 1987, Peter Duesberg had never had a single grant proposal rejected by the Department of Health. Since 1991, he has written a total of 25 research proposals, and not a single one has been accepted. And what had he done? He had refuted the HIV theory. Despite this hounding and intolerance of the government, 2,300 distinguished scientists and doctors, including Nobel Prize winners, have signed the petition of the Group for the Scientific Reappraisal of the HIV-AIDS Hypotheses.

Despite having spent billions of dollars on "fighting AIDS", the government was not successful in demonstrating its HIV theory in the United States, and so they moved abroad, primarily to Black Africa. Many people today have been led to believe that there are millions of people dying of AIDS in Black Africa. That is, of course, nonsense propagated by the World Health Organisation. One must always remember that all the health authorities use the names HIV and AIDS interchangeably, so that when the WHO say two million people are dying of AIDS in Africa, what they mean is two million people have HIV, and it is ASSUMED that, therefore, they will die of AIDS. But they don't.

It is also necessary to remember that Black Africa has very limited medical facilities, and that millions of people die every year of unknown causes. They are, therefore, not in a position even to count how many people have died, let alone diagnose why they have died. The one thing the Africans know is that the only thing that will get them money from the West is AIDS. An example of this was Uganda some years ago, which received US$ 6 million to fight AIDS and US$ 50,000 for everything else. From the number of people who die every year, therefore, the Africans take a large number and report that they have died from AIDS, which obtains them medical funding from the West. And yet everyone knows that malaria kills half of the people who die in Africa every year.

As the African countries do not have the money, or the equipment, for AIDS tests, they use instead the "Bangui" definition of AIDS (established in the city of Bangui in the Central African Republic). This definition considers AIDS is present if there is the presence of chronic diarrhoea, fever, significant weight loss and asthenia. These happen to be the symptoms of almost every illness that exists in Africa. If HIV does not cause AIDS, then AIDS cannot be transmitted sexually, and all the sexual precautions people take are a farce. In Kampala, the prostitutes at the hotels are the same ones who were there 20 years ago. They are not too worried by AIDS.

So why have we had this ridiculous farce, costing billions of dollars? Because the government did not wish to admit that AIDS is a homosexual and drug-users' disease, and was prepared to spend billions of dollars trying to hide this fact. Yet, today, 30 years after the AIDS outbreak in America, homosexuals and drug addicts still make up 80 percent of the victims.

The hustler

In 1973, Bobby Riggs organised the Battle of the Sexes, an exhibition tennis match in which he, a 55 year-old man, would play the No.1 lady player in the world, Margaret Court, who won more major tournaments (24) than any woman player in tennis history. Bobby Riggs had been a gambler and a hustler all his life. When he won Wimbledon in 1939, he had already received reprimands from the tennis authorities for betting on the matches. He later became a professional tennis player — one of the best in the world — and he also took up golf, which he played for big money. He pretended to be a four handicap, but he really played to scratch. One of his tricks when playing in Florida was to wear long-sleeved shirts, so that his opponents would not see how tanned his arms were, and would think he had just come down from the north.

In the Battle of the Sexes, people did not believe a 55 year-old man, no matter how good he had been earlier, would be able to beat the best lady player in the world, and the odds on the match were 2/1 against Riggs. Riggs backed himself heavily and won the match easily: 6-2, 6-1. This naturally upset a lot of women. Two or three months later, Riggs was challenged by Billie Jean King, the No.2 lady player in the world at the time. This time, however, in view of Riggs' triumph against Court, the odds were the opposite: 2/1 on Riggs, and 2/1 against Mrs King. Amazingly, to all those who knew Riggs well, he lost very tamely: 6-4, 6-3, 6-3 to Mrs King, double faulting on match point, something he had never done in his entire career.

The Feminists were now satisfied and, since then, whenever the Battle of the Sexes is mentioned, it is always stated that Mrs King beat Riggs. Amazingly, no one ever mentions that Riggs first beat the No.1 woman, Mrs Court. But those who knew Riggs well (that is, knew not only what a strong competitor he was, but also what a hustler he was), know the reason for the result in the King match. Riggs took the 2-1 odds on King. Having made a bundle backing himself against Miss Court, he made another bundle backing Miss King against himself. After all, it was only an exhibition.

World hypocrisy

Everyone knows that we live in an age of hypocrisy. Now there is nothing new about hypocrisy, it has been with us since the beginning of time. What is new is that the nature of this hypocrisy has altered. The dictionary tells us that hypocrisy is "sham or pretence". In the past such sham or pretence was usually used in support of the institutions of society — the Church, the Army, the State, the aristocracy, society, etc. All these institutions have decreased drastically in importance over the last fifty years, and are now in full retreat. Yet the flow of hypocrisy continues unabated — indeed it is greater than ever. The reason is that hypocrisy has simply changed direction, and the hypocrisy that one hears today is much less about institutions, and much more about individual people. It invariably has to do with individuals trying to justify themselves, even if they have to insult other people's intelligence to do so. Whether it is a cabinet minister refusing to resign after a blunder (refusing even to admit that he has made a blunder); or a girl who batters her mother to death with a hammer and blames it on premenstrual tension; or a law school which awards a graduation degree to a girl who has been caught cheating, while at the same time announcing that, "No one can come to our school, and get away with cheating". At every level of society, the level of hypocrisy today has become shameless.

Another aspect of today's atmosphere is that where in the past hypocrisy was invariably laughed at, (sometimes even by those who were putting it forward), there is very little ridicule today of even the most shameless hypocrisy. Outrageous justifications are taken quite seriously, and even given importance in the press. It is one of the facts of life today that almost all levels of competence have been lowered. From cabinet ministers to street-sweepers, it has become very difficult to find any longer people who know how to do their job properly. This incompetence is inexorably intertwined with the general hypocrisy — instead of having to admit that they have simply been incompetent, everyone now pretends that it was someone else's fault. As they are not laughed at, they continue to do so again and again. Eventually the idea of responsibility for one's actions disappears.

One of the reasons that Socialism is fallacious is that its theories takes no account of human weakness or folly, and it invariably assumes that anyone who finds himself in a disagreeable position must be there because of the fault of others. In short, they deny that there is any such thing as personal responsibility. As it is only human nature to try to avoid fault or responsibility if one can, it is not very difficult to persuade people that nothing is ever their own fault. Nor is it surprising that the bubble of hypocrisy in the modern world is getting bigger and bigger. What is regrettable is that more people do not take the trouble of pricking it with ridicule. That is the one thing against which hypocrisy can not stand.

Even the Royal Family is not immune to hypocrisy; indeed, they specialise in it. The most astounding Royal event took place when Prince Charles stated, on television, to all his subjects, that he had not seen Camilla during the first six years of his marriage. He said that he had not seen her until the marriage "broke down". This was obviously nonsense. If he had not been seeing her, why did the marriage break down? Diana made it very clear that she considered Camilla to be the only obstacle in her marriage. But, secondly, literally thousands of people knew that he had been seeing Camilla. Neither he nor Camilla are discreet. Everyone in their circle knew, and also many others not in their circle. Usually, one lies to avoid people finding out something disagreeable. But, in this case, everyone already knew the disagreeable facts, so Charles was trying to deny something many people knew to be true. That is very arrogant, as well as dishonest.

Another instance of Royal hypocrisy took place when it was reported in the national Press that Princess Diana had been caught making dozens of telephone calls from Kensington Palace to the home of Oliver Hoare, a married man, whose marriage she broke up. When Diana was asked about it, her reaction to the Press was to start crying and say: "Why is everyone picking on me?". Immediately the story disappeared from the Press and the matter was never, ever, heard of again. What kind of free Press is that?

Finally, Diana's accident also was full of hypocrisies. First of all, trying to blame the accident on the chauffeur being "drunk" was absurd. The chauffeur had had two glasses of red wine with his dinner, as he did every night of his life. But that is not the point. The point is that chauffeurs only go as fast as their clients want them to go. If the client wants to go 20 miles-an-hour, the chauffeur drives at 20 miles-an-hour. If they want to go 80, he goes 80. If the car was going very fast, it was because Diana and Dodi wanted him to go fast. But there is still another fact that is even more amazing. Long before the accident, the police had a file on Dodi, because he might have become the future King's stepfather. After the accident, supposedly there was the most intense investigation in police history. Yet it was never announced by the police that Dodi was a cocaine addict, that he had cocaine every night of his life, and that he was almost certainly drugged the night of the accident. That is hypocrisy with a vengeance.

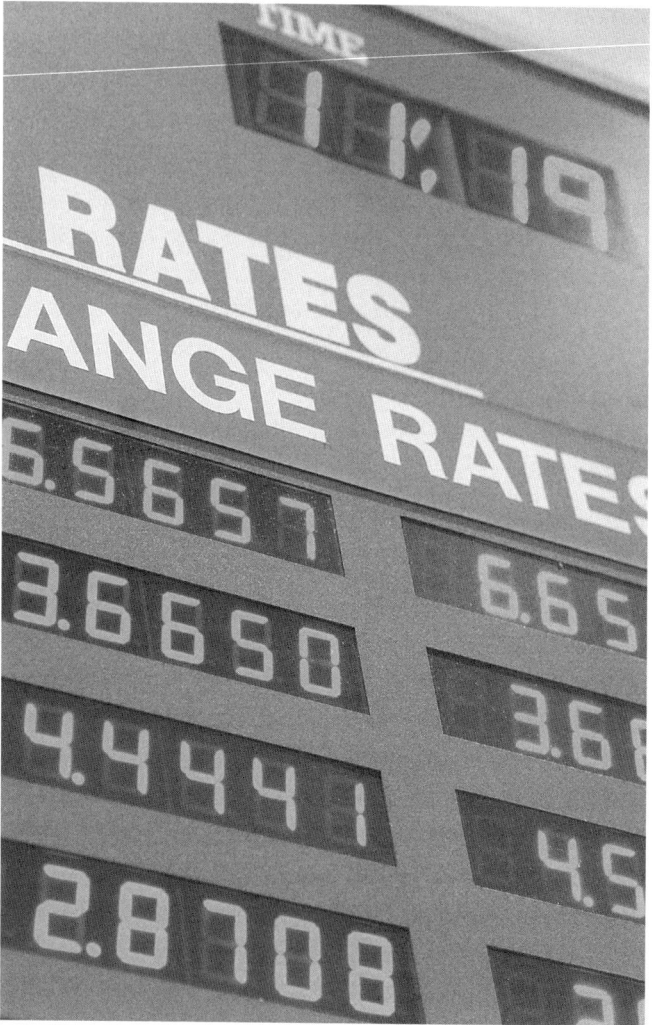

The Crisis

The one thing that is on most people's minds at the moment is the financial crisis. And yet this crisis is a nest of outrageous and interrelated hypocrisies. The most important thing that it necessary to understand is that only the government can cause inflation, and only the government does cause inflation. That is because only the government can increase the amount of money existing at any time. When we hear, as we have often heard, the government promising to "fight inflation", it is so hypocritical that it is nauseating. They are pretending to "fight" with one hand, what they are doing with the other hand.

In the century from the Battle of Waterloo, in 1815, to the beginning of the First World War in 1914, the value of money did not change. During that period, governments did not interfere in the financial markets. Prices rose and fell for short periods, but they always returned to equilibrium. Some banks and enterprises went bankrupt. But the value of money remained the same. A pound in 1914 could buy just as much as a pound in 1815. This is certainly not the case today. In 1952, a three-course dinner, with wine, at The Ritz cost 19/6. Today, it would cost £70 or £80. That is quite a difference. The reason is that in the 20th century, governments began interfering in the financial markets. The U.S. Federal Reserve was established in 1913. The European countries had been bankrupted by the First World War, and after the War their governments began to inflate. During the U.S. Senate Hearings in 1913, on the Federal Reserve Act, Senator Root of New York said on the Senate floor, "This Act is simply an engine for inflation". He has certainly been proved right. The governments like inflation, because it makes people feel richer, and more likely to vote for them, it enables the governments to pay off their debts with debased money. Most of all it enables governments to spend more money and thereby buy more votes.

However, although it is governments that create inflation, it is the markets that reverse inflation, and sometimes even cause deflation. The Western governments all inflated in the 1920s, eventually resulting in the deflation of the 1930s. After the Second World War, the process of inflation began again, especially after 1970. However, there was always a built-in brake to inflation in a free market, namely interest rates, because as inflation continues, so interest rates go up to reflect this. Eventually, interest rates go so high that they break the back of inflation, and the money supply is reversed. This is what happened in 1980-1982, when Paul Volcker was Chairman of the U.S. Federal Reserve, and "squeezed" inflation out of the financial system. But since 1982, and especially in the last dozen years, something extraordinary and unprecedented has happened – namely, although the government inflated again, as usual, this time they did not allow interest rates to go up. They deliberately and artificially kept interest rates down, thus allowing the economic credit bubble to continue expanding. What they did was similar to removing the brake of a car and then driving it faster and faster. They were foolish enough to believe that this would result in continuous prosperity. There could be only one ending. The behaviour of our governments was, of course, unconscionable, and the protestations of the Americans, and of Mr Gordon Brown — our Chancellor of the Exchequer — that they were not responsible are particularly nauseating. The hypocrisy is beyond belief. Yet our Mr Brown refuses to apologise. Even having destroyed our economies, the leaders of the United States and Britain now propose to remedy the situation by continuing (as Mrs Merkel has pointed out) the same policy of expanding money supply and keeping interest rates low. Their stupidity and dishonesty are terrifying.

Beyond the basic cause of the crash, there are interesting details. In 1933, the United States had passed the Glass-Steagall Act, which prohibited commercial banks from dealing in investments, and prohibited investment banks from doing commercial banking activities. This was a very sensible measure, and kept the banks in reasonable order until 1990. Unfortunately, in 1990, this Act was repealed - for reasons best known to the psychiatrists of the legislators. The result of this was that all the big Wall Street brokers now became banks, and took deposits as well as continuing to be brokers, while the big banks started trading and speculating. This was combined with an enormous increase in "leverage" (percentage of borrowed money) by all the banks. Leverage is the ratio of a bank's assets to its capital. Pre-1990, this used to be between seven and ten times. Post-1990, it immediately started ballooning and, although the banks tried to keep the exact figure secret, it was known that Merrill Lynch was more than 40 times, Goldman Sachs was 28 times, and Lehman Brothers was 30 times when it failed. Regardless what one thinks of such hair-raising tactics, the one thing that is clear is that they only work when the market is going up. Apart from their Balance Sheet, all the banks also had an enormous amount of "derivatives", which were kept off the Balance Sheet. Derivatives are a cocktail of very exotic Options, on almost anything. In 1995, I was talking, at a dinner party, to someone rich and supposedly very well connected in the financial world, and I asked him what he thought the total nominal value of derivatives were at that time. He said he thought perhaps $100 billion. In fact, at that time, they were $1 trillion. Today, they are $1.3 quadrillion — all off the Balance Sheet. They are also not included in any bankruptcy. Of course, this is only the nominal value, and the actual amount at risk is much less. But five percent of $1.3 quadrillion is $65 trillion — still a tidy sum.

As you can see, the situation was like a keg of dynamite with a running fuse. The explosion came when the American housing market started falling for the first time since the War. Of course, the weakest part was the "sub prime area", but it all fell. These sort of markets were not in a position to withstand such a shock. One of the problems was that those in power did not know what was going on. In fairness to them, it must be said that it was not easy to grasp all the exotic financial products which the traders were using. Furthermore, as the banks began to do more and more trading, and more and more of their profits came from trading, the traders in the firms took control of the firms away from the bankers. As long as the traders were making a ton of money, it was very hard for the bankers in the firms to object. In other words, all these firms were houses of cards waiting to collapse.

The second step took place when the government declined to bail out Lehman Brothers. This shook up the derivative market, changed all the valuations, and gave a big shock to AIG, the giant insurance company. Because, unfortunately for it, apart from doing insurance business, AIG also had a big property portfolio, and had a lot of sub-prime exposure. The government, as you know, decided AIG was "too big to fail" and, in one day, it reversed the stance that it had taken on Lehman Brothers. This led to the present situation. It is important to understand that the problem is not one of liquidity. The banks have liquidity, and the government is now trying to substitute government liquidity for private liquidity. The problem is one of solvency. The liabilities of these businesses exceed their assets by a considerable amount. That is why it is misguided to say the banks should be bailed out. That will simply prolong the pain indefinitely. The only way the problem can ever been solved is by selling their assets for whatever they can, and writing off the rest. Very painful, but the only way the banking system can regain stability. It is interesting that, ten years ago, there was an investment company in the United States called Long Term Capital, which employed very distinguished people, and was backed by very distinguished people. To begin with, it was very successful, but then they made a blunder, and they went bankrupt. As usual, the government stepped in, said it was "too big to fail", and bailed it out. Of course, the shareholders got nothing. I suggest that if LTC had been allowed to fail in 1998, the excesses that took place later would perhaps not have happened.

It is also important to correct some popular misconceptions about the markets. Firstly, short selling. No sound enterprise has ever been destroyed by short selling. Short sellers only attack firms that are in financial trouble, and likely to go bankrupt. They jump on the bandwagon. "Insider dealing" is another whipping boy of those outside the financial markets. Yet the fact is that insider dealing does not hurt any other investors — there is no victim. The ban on it is based on the envy that people have for others who have more information than they do, and can, therefore, supposedly make more money. Finally, some people state that governments should not let banks fail, because if they do, there is a "loss of trust". I would suggest the opposite — that governments must let banks fail, because only then will other banks start behaving responsibly. If some people lose their money, those are the risks of life. It is up to everyone to choose a sound bank, and not an unsound one. If you ran into someone on the street, who offers to sell you Tower Bridge, and you agreed to give him your money, should you be able later to go to the government and ask to be reimbursed? How is it different if he has a bank, and you give him your money to deposit in his bank? Banks are just commercial enterprises — there is nothing sacred about them.

The nicer guy

'Fascism' is a word that is used very often in the modern world, and yet very few people understand what it means. The Fascist Party was founded by Mussolini in 1919, and its purpose was to fight Communism. So it started on the side of the angels. But once Mussolini took power in Italy, it turned into a violent dictatorship, and the word Fascism came to mean a non-Socialist violent dictatorship. Surprisingly enough, the Nazis were not Fascist — they were Socialists. Indeed, the word 'Nazi' comes from the initials of their party, being the National Socialist Party in German.

Nor were the Nazis anti-Communist. Indeed, they were allies of the Russian Communists, who supplied them with oil. The wave of German tanks that spread all over Western Europe ran on Russian oil. If Hitler had remained allied to the Russians, it is unlikely that England would have been able to hold out alone against Hitler and Stalin, and we would all be speaking German today. However, for reasons best known to his psychiatrist, Hitler invaded Russia and destroyed himself. In the meantime, Mussolini had allied himself with Hitler. So the two allies were called 'the Fascists', although only one of them was Fascist. We were allied with the Communists, but nobody called us Communists. As the War went on, Hitler moved more and more to the Left, and the Nazis became more and more Socialist.

Who was the nicer guy? For the last 60 years, we have been hearing continually about the Nazis and the Holocaust. Although this was a horrible event, it is also one of the biggest hypocrisies in the world. Not because the Holocaust did not take place (of course it did), but because I have never heard a Jew, or even a non-Jew, admit the fact that Stalin killed many more people than Hitler, and many more Jews. It is, nevertheless, a fact.

Estimates of the Nazi concentration camps are that between three and six million people died there. Suppose we take a medium number of four and a half million — of course, all of them were not Jews. Estimates, by Russian experts, of the people murdered by the Russian Communists is between 60 million and 80 million people. Now, it is not possible to tell exactly how many Jews died, not only because the Russians did not have concentration camps where people could be counted and people were killed in different ways or sent to die in Siberia, but also because the Germans killed Jews during a period of four or five years, while the Russians were killing Jews for 30 years. But Jews were an important element in the Russian nation, and they also excelled in politics, and in the arts, and professions. So, of the estimate of between 60 and 80 million people murdered by the Russian Communists, a very large number were Jews.

The situation in Russia was more complicated, because there were many Jews high up in the Communist Party. Stalin, being more intelligent than Hitler, never attacked the Jews openly. But that did not change the fact that there was very strong anti-Semitism in Russia and, in particular, Stalin himself was a violent anti-Semite, who went on quietly killing Jews. The extent of his feelings are shown by the fact that he killed his own friends because they were Jewish; he killed members of his own family because they were Jewish; he even killed ex-mistresses because they were Jewish. It is an interesting reflection on the world that one has never heard any public person state these facts, although we hear about the Holocaust almost every day in the Press. It shows the power of the Left.

Words

In his famous essay "On Language", George Orwell said "Sloppy language leads to sloppy thinking". Socialists understand this very well and, through the use of words, they have been able to manipulate people's idea of reality by using words opposed to their real meaning. One of the most common words in our language today is the word "Capitalism". Yet the word "Capitalism" was invented by Karl Marx in order to try to rubbish the freedom of the West. The word has no meaning because it suggests that our system is based on capital, but in fact it is not. We do not even have a "system". What we have is freedom. But Marx did not like to admit that our way of life was freedom, while the Socialists way was slavery, so he tried to rubbish us by using the word "Capitalism". The amazing thing is that we in the West have embraced this word, which rubbishes us, and we use it continually. It is rather like being told by Joe Bloggs that one is "a son of a bitch", and responding by saying "Yes, I am a son of a bitch, and I will call myself a son of a bitch from now on".

Another such word is "gay". Until 30 years ago, this word had never been used about homosexuality. In the nineteenth century, it was used regarding prostitutes. Now, there are a dozen words in the English language — some correct English and some slang — which mean homosexual. And yet from the moment that the word "gay" was introduced, everyone uses only the word "gay", and anyone who uses any other word is criticized. If there is nothing wrong with homosexuality, as many people in the Anglo-Saxon world now pretend, why is it necessary to use the euphemism "gay"? How was this imposed on the world? Certainly by the media, and the Left. Suppose for the last 30 years, homosexuals had been referred to as pederasts, which is a correct English word. Would homosexuals have the same importance and the same influence that they have today? That is why words are so important, and that is why the Left has been so successful.

When Lenin died in 1924, the London Times, the most respected newspaper in the world at the time, printed an obituary. The title of the obituary was "Gospel of Hate". In 1924, everyone knew that Socialism was a gospel of hate, but today not only do people not think so, but we are governed by people who are filled with hate. It is an amazing achievement by the Socialists.

Perfidious Albion

In 1998, the Ministry of Defence invited a delegation from Chile to visit manufacturers of military weapons in England and to, hopefully, buy some. The MoD paid for their flights, arranged their itinerary, and met them at the airport. The leader of the delegation was General Pinochet, Chief-of-Staff of the Chilean Armed Forces, and previously President for 15 years. Having retired as President in 1989, General Pinochet then ran for office in the next elections. He did not win, but he received 43 percent of the votes, which is more than Mrs Thatcher ever received. When their tour was over, most of the Chileans went back to Chile, but because General Pinochet had a bad back and needed a small operation, he decided to stay in England and have it done here.

In order to understand what was about to happen, one must know something about Chilean history. Although Chile had always been a Christian Democratic country, in 1970 there were two Christian Democratic candidates, who split the CD vote, and allowed Salvador Allende to be elected. Allende is usually referred to as a "Socialist" by the Western press but, in fact, Allende was Head of the Chilean Communist Party, which fact he did not try to hide. He openly declared himself in favour of a violent revolution. Because he was the most charismatic on the Left, the Socialists allied themselves with him. In the fourth year of his four-year term, it was clear that Allende would not be re-elected. He had destroyed Chile; the inflation rate was 600 percent; and Communist gangs roamed the countryside. Obviously, no one was interested in displacing Allende violently, as he would be displaced automatically in a few months.

Allende, however, did not wish to be displaced. He was a traitor and he brought 15,000 Cuban troops into Chile. Together with his Chilean Communist troops, he hoped to take power by force. That was the background of the Chilean Civil War, which ended with Allende dead, and Pinochet in power. Pinochet restored order and not only lowered the inflation rate, but made Chile an economic model for all of South America. Of course, Pinochet was very unpopular with the Left, because he had made fools of them, and they immediately started to allege torture. Now, whenever and wherever the Communists are defeated and sent to jail, they automatically allege torture. They did it in Malaya, they did it in Greece, they did it in Spain, and they did it in Chile. The point of alleging torture is, first of all, it sounds horrible and, more importantly, it cannot be disproved — you cannot prove a negative. Some of the mud always sticks.

At the time that General Pinochet was in England, a Spanish Communist Judge called Garzon was preparing a case against him, with which he hoped to extradite him from England. Now, there was no legal way that Garzon could have extradited Pinochet, because the supposed "crime" took place in Chile, Pinochet was in England and Garzon was in Spain. It was as if the English claimed the right to extradite people from China who had committed a crime in India. However, Garzon had something up his sleeve. In one of the absurd International Human Rights Conventions, there is a statement (not legal of course) that anyone who has committed "genocide" can be extradited by any country. Of course, there had been no genocide in Chile, so this was absurd, but Judge Garzon, in his documents, claimed that General Pinochet had killed all the Communists, and that that was equivalent to genocide. Even more absurd.

While this was going on, General Pinochet had gone into the hospital. His aides had heard about the Spanish Judge Garzon, and they asked the Ministry of Defence and the Foreign Office whether Pinochet was in any danger. Both of them confirmed that Pinochet was in no danger whatsoever. On October 2nd, his aides asked the MoD and F.O. again, and were told again that he was not in any danger. By October 15th, the rumours continued and, again, Pinochet's aides consulted the MoD and the F.O., and were assured that Pinochet was not in any danger. The third lie.

The next day, October 16th, Pinochet was arrested. Treachery. There were quite a few things about this arrest that were defective. First of all, Pinochet had been a former Head of State and ally of Mrs Thatcher's; he was invited and brought to England by the MoD; he had stayed in England for medical reasons; and Judge Garzon's request for extradition had no basis. But there was still another reason why this request for extradition was faulty — it was technically "illegal", because Judge Garzon had not written it properly. At this point, the English Government actually interfered. Garzon's request for extradition was returned to Spain, to be corrected, and the Crown Prosecution Service went to Spain with it, in order to teach Garzon how to do it properly. The Crown Prosecution Service exists to prosecute cases in the U.K. on behalf of foreign countries. It was unheard of for it to actually go to a foreign country and actually write the extradition Order for them. Garzon sent the Crown Prosecution Service to Juan Garces, a well-known Communist and friend of Allende's, who had been with Allende when the Presidential Palace in Chile was burned. The worst treachery was that, during the six days that Garzon's Extradition Order was being corrected, there was nothing holding Pinochet in the U.K. any more. He was free to go. But neither the MoD nor the F.O. told him so. They kept him in the U.K. on false pretences. What sort of government is that?

When the corrected Extradition Order finally arrived, the Home Secretary, Mr Jack Straw, refused the many petitions for Pinochet's release, and pretended that he would have to let the matter go to court, because there was "nothing else" he could do. Yet, a year before, when Germany had asked for the extradition of an IRA bomber, who had committed violent acts in Germany, Mr Straw refused to hand her over. He claimed she was pregnant, and pretended that she might suffer from PMT. An IRA bomber! Another example of Mr Straw's "honesty" involved the female spy Miss Norwood, who was found to have passed nuclear secrets to the Russians throughout the Cold War. Straw decided not to even try her, let alone put her in jail.

Another lunacy was that by law, in Spain, no one was allowed to go to jail over the age of 80. As Pinochet was 82, he obviously could never go to jail in Spain. So what was all the fuss about? Obviously, the Left simply wanted a show trial for propaganda. During the trial in the Law Lords which followed, Pinochet was kept under house arrest.

Not long afterwards, the Chinese Communist leaders visited England. The Chinese Communists, as people who are familiar with the Orient know, butchered not millions, but tens of millions of their own people. But when they came to London, they had tea with the Queen in Buckingham Palace, while Pinochet, who saved Chile from Communism, was under arrest.

Perfidious Albion indeed.

Let's have a date for rape

One hears continuous complaints by Feminists that not enough men are being convicted of "date rape". The reason that men are not convicted of date rape is that there is no such thing as "date rape". There is only rape. The crucial elements of rape are that the woman is unwilling, and that the man commits a violent act. These elements are always the same, whether an act is committed by a stranger in the bushes, or by someone one knows, in one's flat. The fact that you know the man makes no difference whatsoever.

Of men tried for rape about 44% are convicted, which is similar to the percentage of convictions in other countries, and also the percentage of convictions of other crimes. What Feminists complain about is that only one out of seven alleged rapes ever go to court. That is, of course, because the "alleged rapes" are mainly in the minds of the women alleging them, and once they come into contact with the police, they are quickly dropped. Indeed, it is the Feminists themselves who are at fault in causing this wave of imaginary rapes, because they have led women to believe that, if they make love to a man and it was not satisfactory, it must have been "rape".

But there is another point which is crucial, but which no one ever mentions. Allegations of rape only occur between men and women who do not know each other very well, and who have never been to bed with each other before. Couples who are established lovers are not in the habit of alleging rape. Furthermore, people do not usually make love in the street, or in the park — it is invariably in somebody's flat. That means that the young lady in question either agreed to go to the young man's flat, or else actually invited him to her flat. To do this with a stranger, who has invariably had a few drinks, is insane behaviour, unless, of course, the girl wants to make love. How can there be rape in such circumstances?

Sexual harassment One of the most absurd hypocrisies in the world today is the recent phenomenon of "sexual harassment". All Feminists believe implicitly, and state vehemently, that women are "equal" to men. What "equal" means is not very clear. Are a dog and a cat "equal"? Are a lion and an elephant "equal"? An objective observer would say "No, of course not. They are both animals, but they are different animals". Similarly, a man and a woman are both human beings, but they are different human beings.

Now, Feminists insist that women can do anything that men can do. Not only work in an office, but be soldiers, sailors, policemen, be fireman, etc. And yet, at the same time, they state that women can be "sexually harassed" by men. How can one be "harassed" by someone who is equal to you? Men never complain about "sexual harassment". How can women soldiers and sailors face the enemy if they can not deal with "sexual harrassment"? This is really one of the most absurd ideas of the century. If women are equal, they cannot complain about being treated like a man. If they want to be fragile little flowers and be protected, then they cannot pretend that they are "equal" to men. And yet this absurd idea has existed for 30 years or more, and no one says anything about it. This is hypocrisy with a vengeance.

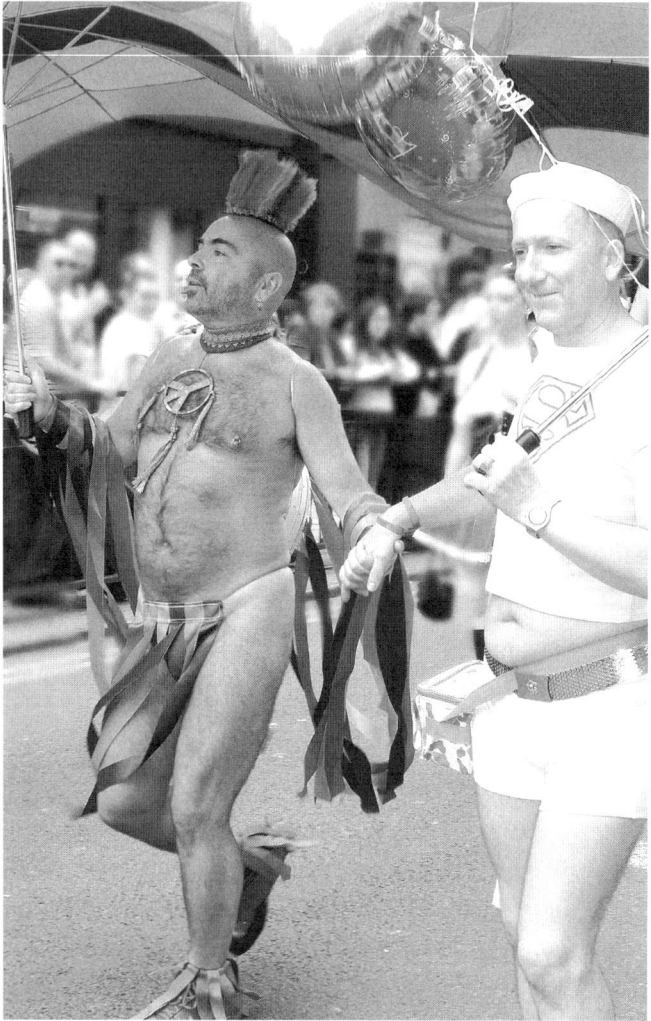

How gay is my valley

Since 1965 homosexuality has been legal and therefore tolerated in this country. But it is necessary to understand that the homosexual community are not satisfied with having their homosexuality tolerated by the rest of the country — they also want it to be approved. This, of course, makes no sense, because if there is nothing wrong with homosexuality, as they insist, why do they wish to be approved? But they do wish it — very much. In order to accomplish this, they have to spin a fantasy about homosexual life, which has nothing to do with reality. Homosexuals do not live in rose-covered cottages, with one of them wearing an apron and cooking dinner, and the other reading his paper in front of the television. Homosexuals sometimes live together, but they do not live together as man and wife. They live together as room-mates, and both of them go out cruising. And when they go cruising, they find five, ten or 15 different partners. It is important to remember that they are far more promiscuous than normal people. That is why they need drugs.

Furthermore, there is a very disagreeable side to homosexuality, which is never mentioned. At American universities, the loos had to be closed, because the homosexuals drilled holes in each partition, so they could watch their neighbour. There are bars in New York where there are plywood partitions with holes in them, and homosexuals put their cocks in without even knowing who is on the other side. Or, they put their bottoms up to the hole, and some stranger on the other side hammers them. The attempts to try and equate homosexual life with normal life is absurd. Yet that is what they are trying to persuade us to think.

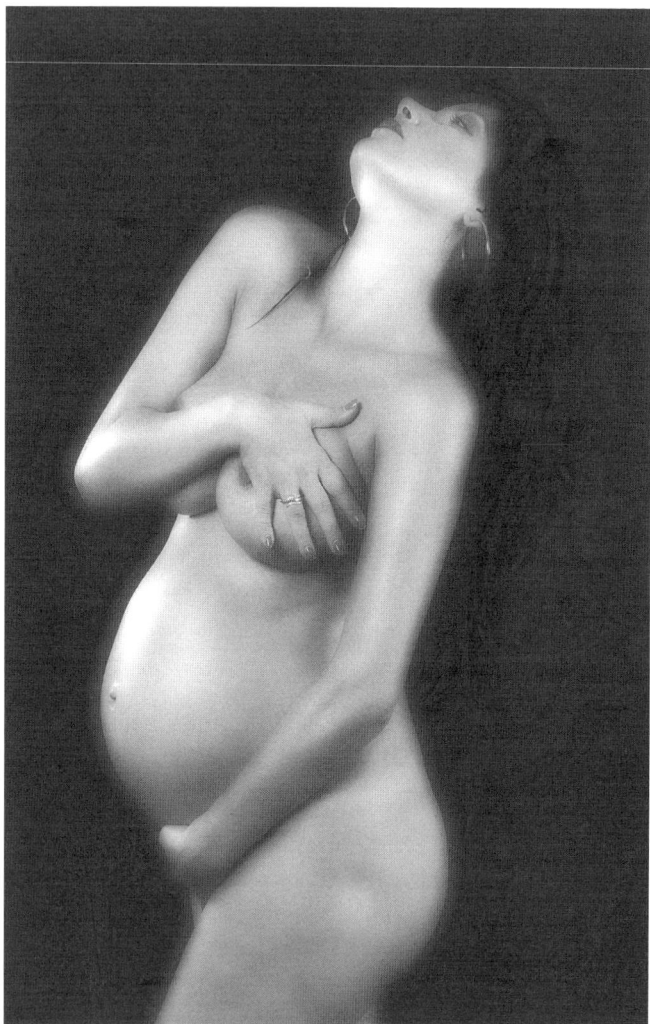

A crisis of love

We live in a world where we are continuously being threatened with all kinds of dangers: global warming, AIDS, etc. All of them are completely false. But there is something that really is threatening us, which is never, ever, mentioned, and yet it has to do with the continuance of the European race.

About 30 years ago, there was a survey done in France, concerning the incidence of love-making. At that time, married couples made love about eight times a month, or twice a week. That was what most people would have guessed. A couple of years ago, there was another survey. This time they found that married couples now made love once a month. In other words, in France, the home of *l'amour toujours*, love-making has fallen by 90% in the last 25 years. As far as unmarried people are concerned, 15% of those surveyed had not made love for more than a year. Those are amazing results. A recent German survey showed similar results — people are not making love any more. In Germany, as a consequence, the birth rate has fallen drastically, and the German government are now paying people to have babies.

In the U.K. there was an even more surprising survey, during the last World Cup. British youths were asked what they would rather do: make love to the woman of their dreams (not their girlfriends, but the woman of their dreams), or watch the World Cup on television. Ninety-five percent said they would prefer to watch the World Cup. In the previous generation, it would have been the other way around — 95% would have preferred to make love to the woman of their dreams. Another frightening thing, which has recently been made public, is that the sperm count in men is falling drastically. In the past, men had an average sperm count of 75 million. It is now only 55 million - in other words, it has fallen by 30 percent. Yet, in order to have a child, the minimum sperm count is 35 million. So we are half way to not being able to have children. Yet nobody talks about these things.

I would suggest that there are two main reasons for the fall in love-making. The first is to do with women working. Without criticising women working, the fact is that when women work, that is bad for love-making. The woman comes home tired, and then has to cook dinner, see to chores about the house, look after the children etc. By the time she goes to bed, she is exhausted. So when the husband wants some action, perhaps she pushes him away. This is very bad for their relationship. Next time, the man may not try or he may not try for a while. When he does try, perhaps she will feel that she had better not reject him again, but as she is exhausted, the love-making will not be very good. This is destructive of their physical relationship and leads to a vicious circle. But it seems today that people are more interested in how many things they can buy, and how much money they can make, rather than what kind of relationship they have. When women started working, many people thought that it would not catch on in the Latin countries, where men expect women to look after them. But, in fact, women went to work just as much in the Latin countries, because the men wanted the money. The only difference was that they were expected to look after the men as well as work.

The other reason for the decline in love-making has to do with aiming to please. Since time immemorial, human beings have always aimed to please. That is what human intercourse is about. One aims to please. Women particularly have tried to please men, because women need husbands. Clever women know that the more a woman pleases a man, the better their love-life will be, and the stronger the bond between them. Today there is no aim to please — on the contrary, there is only an aim to displease. Women have the idea that men are like light switches: when one wants power, one just flicks the switch. Many women don't understand that men have feelings, desires, moods, etc. Above all, they don't understand that there is a part of the man's body that does not follow instructions — it does what it wants. They don't grasp this. There was recently a survey of "yobbos". These are the young boys wandering around the streets in dirty jeans, sweat-shirts and orange hair. The interviewers asked them whether they wanted their girlfriends to look like them or whether they wanted their girlfriends to look nice. Ninety-five percent said they would like their girlfriends to look nice. But their girlfriends did not get it — they still look a mess.

There is a well-known story in Paris, about an aristocratic lady, who had been a widow for some time. She had always had a very indifferent lovelife — in fact, she had never had a climax in her life. One day, a man came into her life, who courted her. Eventually they made love, and the very first time they made love she had a climax — her first. One would think she would have grasped the man with both hands and not let him go. But not so. The next time they met, as he was driving her home, he said "I would like you to wear stockings, because I hate tights". "Oh, yes", she said, "I will do that for you". Unfortunately, she had had rather a lot to drink at dinner, and the next morning she could not remember the conversation. Two days later, he came to see her, bringing some stockings. She started shouting and abusing him. Naturally, that was the end of the affair. No other man ever appeared who could give her a climax, or who even wanted to make love to her. In Paris she is called "The Lady of One Delight".

Another problem today is that, sometimes, women will not wear things to attract men. For example, scent. They say there is something wrong with scent — that it is artificial. Yet lipstick and rouge, and painted fingernails, are artificial, but they do not worry them. I noticed that an English lady I knew didn't wear scent. I told her "You must start wearing scent. All civilised women wear scent". She replied "It's rather difficult. When I got married, my husband asked me to wear scent and I refused. He would think it odd if I started wearing scent now". It is astonishing that a respectable and high-class woman would refuse to wear scent for her husband, and equally astonishing that her husband would accept this and do nothing about it. There are other ways in which women do not please. When women get older, they often cut their hair — it makes them look older and much less attractive. When one asks them why, they say "It is easier". But life is not about things being easier — it is about being beautiful.

If a man were to shave his head, because it was "easier", women would not be very impressed.

The most significant feature of women's attire today is trousers, and women don't think twice about wearing them. Yet, in the past, wearing clothes of the opposite sex was considered a major sin. In the Bible, it was referred to as an "abomination" (*Deuteronomy 22*). In the Middle Ages, it was a crime, punishable by death. Yet no woman today, when she puts on trousers, thinks that 300 years ago she would have been beheaded for doing so. The point is that as people in the past took the matter very seriously, they must have had some reason for taking the matter seriously. They obviously thought it was inherently repugnant.

Regardless of what one thinks about trousers on women, the fact that cannot be denied is that the only point of trousers is to make women look like men. Is that a good idea? If men wore skirts and stockings, they would be considered transvestites. The fact is that no one cares about men looking like women, but a lot of people want women to look like men. Indeed, women have been persuaded that the only way they can be "equal" is to be dressed like men. This is idiotic. All the famous women in history were dressed like women, not like men. Trousers are made for men, whose bodies are straight up and down, not for women who have curves.

Women who are the slightest bit fat or overweight look terrible in trousers, but very thin women also don't look good in trousers. There is no point saying that Greta Garbo or Audrey Hepburn looked alright in trousers — that does not help the other three billion women in the world. By definition, trousers can not be feminine, nor sexy. In short, trousers do not give men erections. But today, women are not interested in arousing men. Thirty years ago, women wore both trousers and skirts, and there was some pretence of women trying to look nice. But today trousers are worn every day by all women. They have become a uniform. Women no longer even pretend that they want to look nice. They all want to look like the Chinese Red Guards.

Marriage and divorce can not but be affected by these trends. The stronger the lovelife is, the stronger is the marriage. If there is no lovelife, the marriage comes apart very easily. As Anglo-Saxon women (Americans and English) don't aim to please, they have the highest divorce rates. America has the highest divorce rate in the world, and England has the highest in Europe. At the same time, the marriage rate is falling everywhere. In the U.K., it is now below 50 percent — the lowest it has been in history. A lot of people now think that cohabiting is the answer — the best solution. There are more cohabitees than people in marriages. They, too, don't grasp the point. The essence of marriage is a promise — one promises to look after the other person for life — and anyone who breaks his word and does not do so is considered a bad person. When cohabiting, there are no promises or commitment. You can take your toothbrush and leave any time. In America recently, I saw an old friend, who was living with a woman, and I said to him: "You are not getting any younger. Why don't you marry her?" He replied "There is much less downside this way". Six months later, she was gone. There is also the problem that cohabiting produces a lot of little bastards. What happens to them in later life? The Bible (*Deuteronomy 23*) says "A bastard shall not enter into the congregation of the Lord". How do parents deal with this? None of this is good news for the birth rate.

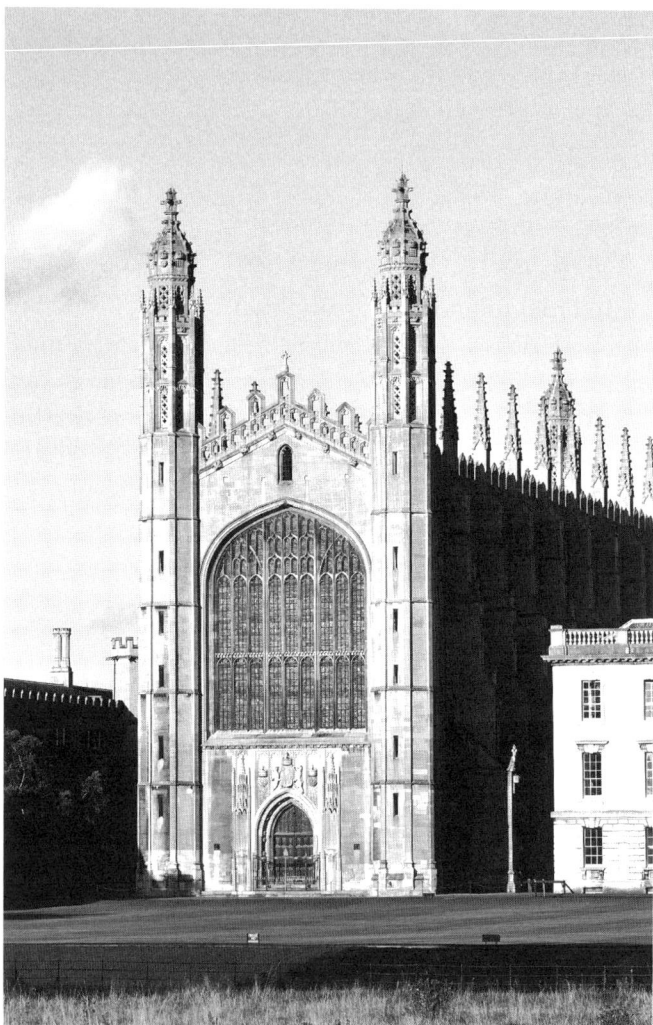

Higher education

In order to understand anything about education in the U.K., it is necessary to grasp that the educational system, which used to be the best in Europe, is now the worst in Europe. This has happened because the educational establishment has been infiltrated by Left-wing people, not only teachers but also administrators, who have consistently and continuously dumbed-down the level of education, while at the same time they have brainwashed the pupils with Left-wing propaganda. Nevertheless, the government has forced universities to accept more and more state school students, even though they are completely unqualified. At Cambridge at the moment, 57% of students come from state schools.

A couple of years ago, I had lunch in Cambridge with four distinguished Cambridge dons. During the course of the lunch, one of them said to me "Half of my students do not know what they are doing — they have no business being here". Somewhat surprised,

I asked the other dons what they thought. They said three-quarters of their students had no business being there. I then asked them how many of these unqualified students would receive degrees. "Oh, we do not fail anyone at Cambridge any more" they all replied. In other words, the government ruthlessly deceives the people by not allowing universities to fail anybody, because, if they did allow them to, then all the state school students would fail, and everyone would see how appalling the state school system is.

At the moment, about 30% of state school students go to university, and the government wants to increase this percentage to 50%. In contrast, on the Continent, every state school student is free to go to university, as long as he has a school certificate. He may not go to the university of his choice, but he will be accepted at some university. But there is a very big difference with England, because the students are severely tested during the course of their studying, and of those who begin university, only one-third receive a degree. Needless to say, English university degrees are not given much importance on the Continent. In the meantime, the Government keeps on pretending that state school students are educated.

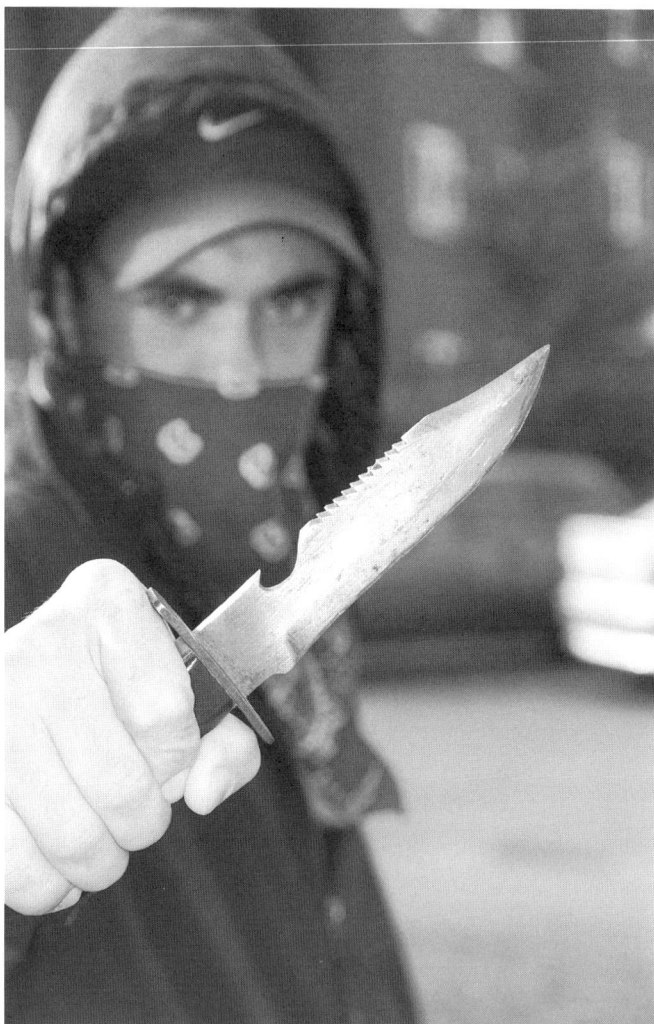

Counting criminals

One of the most extraordinary things that happen in this country is how the government measures crime. One would think this is a perfectly easy thing to do by the records of the Police and/or the Home Office. Yet that is not the way it happens in the U.K. The government recently announced that crime had fallen by 44% in the last ten years. But the figures from the Police and the Home Office showed that crime had gone up by 21% in the last ten years. How can one explain this difference?

Well, one has to do some investigating, but, if one does, one finds out that the government figures come from a company in the Midlands called the British Crime Survey, or BCS. What this enterprise does is to interview 40,000 homes and to ask them how many crimes they are aware have taken place, including crimes that have not been reported. On the basis of these figures, they then try to estimate the total figure of crimes in the country. This is, of course, scandalous.

Anybody can see that. Yet the government goes on ignoring the Police figures and taking their figures from the BCS. There is only one conclusion — the government wish to hide the total number of crimes in this country, in which we are the second in Europe.

This then enables them to pretend that it is not necessary to build more jails in this country — jails being a "No No" to the Left. It is necessary to understand that, as far as the Left are concerned, criminals do not exist. If anyone goes wrong, it is because of his environment and society. Evil does not exist for the Left. Not only is this obvious nonsense, but it is insulting, because it suggests that those of us who are not criminals, are not criminals only because of our environment, and that if we had a different environment, we would be criminals too. It is by this fantasy that the government thinks they can control crime.

Macedonia

Someone looking at a map of South-East Europe might be excused for being puzzled by the fact that there seems to be two Macedonias. As everyone who has any kind of classical education knows, Macedonia, the country of Alexander the Great, has always been a part of Greece. Yet, in what used to be Yugoslavia, there is another country that calls itself Macedonia. This is rather like the French renaming Normandy, and calling it Sussex.

As usual, there is a complicated story behind this strange phenomenon. One has to understand that it is only 100 years since the Balkans became free of Turkey, and there have been several wars since then between Greece, Yugoslavia and Bulgaria about the borders. As long ago as 1893, the Yugoslavs founded an organisation called IMRO (the Internal Macedonian Revolutionary Organisation), whose purpose was to seize Greek territory, and the Bulgarians founded a similar organisation the following year. Since then there has been continuous friction about the borders between these countries. In particular, the Yugoslavs and the Bulgarians have been trying to pretend that Macedonia overlapped into their countries and that, therefore, they want to "liberate" Macedonia, which means seizing territory from the Greeks. Of course, this is without any foundation, because Ancient Macedonia lay entirely within the present day borders of Greece. Furthermore, the Macedonians were Greek, and spoke Greek, whereas the southern Yugoslavs — who were called "Paeonians" — spoke a language called "Paeonian".

Nevertheless, this friction has been going on for many years, and during the War, Tito saw a chance to seize some Greek territory. The majority of the Greek guerrillas were Communists, who intended to take over Greece by force after the War. Tito therefore promised them help to take over Greece, if they gave up part of Macedonia when they did so, which they agreed to do. This was, of course, treason. Fortunately for Greece, after the War Churchill made the Communist guerrillas lay down their arms. Greece was saved, and Macedonia remained intact. However, in order to continue his aggressive intentions, Tito renamed the southernmost province of Yugoslavia "Macedonia". Now that this province has become independent, we have a country called "Macedonia", entirely OUTSIDE OF Greece.

And, instead of telling the Yugoslavs to behave themselves, the Allies have done nothing about it. The hypocrisy of both is outrageous.

Legality and morality

One of the important principles of life and of law is not very well understood in the Anglo-Saxon countries — that is the difference between legality and morality. If you park your car in a no-parking zone, that is illegal, but it is not immoral. Similarly, if you betray your greatest friend, that is immoral, but it is not illegal. This distinction must be kept well in mind; otherwise, reality becomes confused. Thus, for example, in 1965, homosexuality was made legal, because many people, including myself, thought that if Michelangelo and Leonardo had spent their lives in jail, the world would have been a much poorer place. But that did not mean that homosexuality should suddenly became moral. Homosexuality has been a major sin, not only in the Christian religion, but in every religion, for thousands of years. This could not possibly change because of a law passed by a government.

Another very important matter, on which there is

considerable confusion, is taxation. Now, taxation has existed ever since there have been governments, but there have been countless different forms of taxation. In medieval days, one lived in a gangster-like atmosphere, where force prevailed. But from the Renaissance onwards, when people became more civilised, taxation too became more civilised. Many taxes one could choose to avoid. For example, there was a tax on salt — one did not have to eat salt if one did not wish to pay the tax. There was a tax on sugar — again, one was free not to eat it. There were taxes on imports — but, again, one did not have to import anything.

In 1842, Sir Robert Peel introduced the first legal income tax in England. This was the first tax since barbarian times, where the government simply took as much of its citizens' money as it wanted, and the citizens had no way to defend themselves. By the turn of the century, most European countries had jumped on the band wagon and passed an income tax. It was a new way of raising money to finance increasing government expenditure. The United States did not have an income tax until 1913 and, in order to do so, they had to amend their Constitution, because an income tax was against the principles of the Constitution. Of course, these income taxes were introduced the traditional way by starting them very low, so that people would get used to them, and later slowly raising them. In the United States taxes jumped under Roosevelt. Indeed, in his inaugural address in 1933, Mr Roosevelt referred to the "unscrupulous money-changers", and the "temple of our civilisation", which he suggested should be "restored to the ancient truths". He went on to say that the measure of that restoration lay in the extent to which "we apply social values more noble than mere monetary profit". Leaving aside the question of who was to decide what is "more noble", what he is obviously saying is that other people will decide how our money is spent. This compares with President Calvin Coolidge's statement, in 1924, that "The power to tax is the power to destroy", and that the power to take a certain amount of his income is only another way of saying that, for a certain proportion of his time, a citizen must work for the government". In other words, be a slave. In the UK, the Socialists raised taxes drastically after the War. The level of taxes is continually being changed, which makes clear how arbitrary they are.

Without going into the pros and cons of the income tax, the point is that taxes may be legal, but they are not in any way moral. Indeed, as was stated in the view of the American Founding Fathers, an income tax was immoral. In short, there is no moral principle that one should pay income taxes. There is only the fact that there are laws, and that one will be punished if one does not pay. This is understood much better on the Continent. Europeans, and especially Latins, who have much longer civilisations and much more sophistication than the Anglo-Saxons, look at it somewhat differently. They know very well that their governments are corrupt and incompetent, and they know very well that any taxes they pay are going to be lost by incompetence, or used by the government to buy votes and to keep themselves in power. In Renaissance days, kings and emperors kept themselves in power with armies. The armies were not conscripts, but mercenaries, and they had to be paid. So the taxes raised by the kings and emperors of those days were used to pay their armies, and thus keep themselves in power. Today, governments use tax receipts to buy votes, and keep themselves in power. *Plus ça change.*

There was an amusing article in the Sunday papers recently, about the contrasting attitude of the English and the Latins. It suggested that if an Englishman learned, or suspected, that his neighbour was somehow avoiding tax, he would immediately report him to the Inland Revenue. By contrast, if an Italian thought his neighbour was avoiding tax, he would say "Let's find out how he does it, so we can do it too". Indeed, in Latin countries, the amount of tax that companies pay is often decided by negotiation with the Revenue authorities.

Gender hypocrisy

One of the strangest hypocrisies in the world is the belief, held by a large part of the Western world, that men and women are indistinguishable beings, and that they share the same qualities and abilities. Thousands of years of human experience has shown us that this is nonsense and, indeed, our own eyes and ears show us that this is nonsense. But not only does the "politically correct" part of the world believe this, but even many people who are not "politically correct", are not prepared to resist this idea.

Yet it is clear that this idea is opposed to reality. Looking first at some of the physical differences between men and women, men do not have "the Curse"; men do not have babies; men do not have breasts, men do not feed their children by their breasts. Women do not have physical courage. Nor do women have a fraction of the physical strength of men. Women also have big differences on the emotional side. Women's minds work by their emotions. They respond less to facts and logic. That is why men and women do not understand each other very well. If women become upset for any reason, they immediately start crying. This is very effective, because men do not know what to do when women cry, but men do not respect it.

Then there is the question of intelligence. Many tests have shown that the average I.Q.s of men and women is exactly the same. But within that standard there are many differences of distribution and of particular abilities. For example, men have a much wider range of IQs. In other words, geniuses and idiots tend to be men. Women's IQs tend to be closer to the median. Perhaps nature does not want women to be too stupid, because they will then not be able to look after their children. Nor does it want women to be too intelligent, because then they will not be interested in looking after their children. In tests involving words, women do better than men. Women also think much faster than men, although not necessarily more accurately. But in, say, spatial relations, women are no good at all. That is why there are very few women engineers – it is not because they are not allowed to be engineers, it is because they are no good at it. That is also why they are not as good as men at chess. Another example is bridge, which is played by more women than men, and at the middle levels, women are more reliable than men. But at the top levels women cannot play with men.

There is also a big difference in sexual relations. Women who have a good lover will be much more affected by his love-making than the man will be affected by the lovemaking — both physically and emotionally. Unfortunately, satisfactory love-making between men and women is continually declining. Firstly, because the incidence of love-making in the Western world is declining, but, secondly, because the quality of love-making is deteriorating. More and more men have become wimps, and wimps can't make love properly.

The differences between men and women are enormous, and yet a large part of the world pretends that there is no difference between women and men, and we see, today, women soldiers, women sailors, women policemen, women firemen. Many feminists even pretend that there should be "parity" in every sphere. In other words, the numbers of men and women in any occupation should be the same. As the number of men who wish to go into many occupations is many more than women, such "parity" is impossible. What is baffling is how all this has happened. All the feminist laws that have been passed, were passed and accepted by men. Why did they accept things that are against nature and against logic, one wonders? Clearly, normal men are decreasing, and wimps are on the war path.

Picture credits:

facing p1 upper: US Navy / Gary Lucken, fotoLibra; facing p1 lower: Ed Zirkle, fotoLibra; p8: Robert Ho, fotoLibra; p12 (manipulated image): Izzeddeen M. Al Karajeh, fotoLibra; p16: Rob Weaver, fotoLibra; p22: Mark Gillett, fotoLibra; p28: Glyn Thomas, fotoLibra; p32: Henry Griffin, AP Photo; p36: Mikael Svensson, fotoLibra; p42: Einar Borchsenius, fotoLibra; p48: AP/Press Association Images; p52 upper: Barrie Harwood, fotoLibra; p52 lower: Barrie Harwood, fotoLibra; p58: Edward Cooper, fotoLibra; p68 upper: Norman Kelly, fotoLibra; p68 lower: Norman Kelly, fotoLibra; p72: Joseph Banks, fotoLibra; p76 Santiago Llanquin, AP Photo; p84 Franz Roth, fotoLibra; p88: Miles Lewis Davies, fotoLibra; p92: Damir Key Klaic, fotoLibra; p102: Alistair Laming, fotoLibra; p106: John Powell, fotoLibra; p110: Nace Georgi Popov, fotoLibra; p114 upper: Rhonda O'Brien, fotoLibra; p114 lower: Alex Dudley, fotoLibra; p120 upper: Gary Lucken, fotoLibra; p120 lower: David Green, fotoLibra.